Table of Contents

Preface

Who This Book is For

This book is for young minds—perhaps a bit unconventional but still full of potential—the dreamers, the thinkers, and even those with pink or green hair who might currently see the world through a lens tinted by liberal and woke perspectives, whether they realize it or not. It's for those who believe in social justice, inclusivity, and change but might not understand the broader implications of their current beliefs. This book aims to provoke thought and inspire action by showing how unchecked liberalism and a nonchalant attitude towards radical movements could lead to the erosion of the Western way of life we all cherish.

What You Will Get Out of It

By reading this book, you will:

- See the Bigger Picture: Understand how the current trends in liberalism and woke culture might lead to unintended and potentially disastrous consequences.
- Challenge Your Beliefs: Be prepared to question what you've been taught and see things from a new perspective.
- Take Action Learn how you can actively participate in preserving the values and traditions that have made Western nations desirable and prosperous.

- Inspire Change: Find out how you can be part of a
movement that holds politicians accountable and
ensures that our societies do not lose their way.

My Perspective

Picture this: I'm just an everyday person, like you, but with a knack for seeing through the fluff. Imagine the world as your favorite video game—only now, the NPCs (that's non-playable characters, for the uninitiated) are running the show. And guess what? They're terrible at it! Think of politicians who couldn't manage a group project in high school, let alone a nation. It's like watching a comedy where everyone's the butt of the joke, but the punchline is our way of life disappearing. My mission? To hit pause on this crazy game, save our world from the domination of radical ideologies, and keep the Western values we all secretly love, even if we won't admit it.

Main Themes

In this book, you will discover:

- The Trap of Liberalism and Wokism: How these
ideologies might have ensnared well-meaning
individuals and why it's not too late to reverse
decades of post-war liberalism.
- The Importance of Action: Why it's crucial to become
politically active in the right movements, read
political manifestos, and hold leaders
accountable.

-      The Value of Our Heritage: Understand that
       preserving our traditions and values has nothing
       to do with race or ethnicity. This book is not for
       bigots or racists but for those who recognize that
       our traditions and values are the bedrock of our
       ethics and societal success.

The Urgency

We are at a crossroads. If we do not act now, the world as
we know it might come to an end within a few generations.
The liberal, woke attitudes and the nonchalant acceptance
of radical ideologies could lead to the erosion of the very
freedoms and lifestyles that make our nations desirable.
Supporting groups like Hamas, a terrorist organization,
and adopting radical ideologies in the name of inclusivity is
not just wrong but foolhardy.

Conclusion

This book is a call to action. Written in a simple clear way,
yet deeply serious exploration of how to protect and
cherish the Western values that have given us freedom,
prosperity, and a unique cultural identity. Even if you are
an atheist, it's crucial to understand that upholding
Christian values doesn't mean you have to believe in
Jesus. Rather, whether you realize it or not, much of what
you know historically and culturally, as well as your sense
of morality and ethics, derives from the Judaeo-Christian
tradition. These values form the bedrock of our civilization
and have made our nations the most desirable and
ethically sound destinations on the planet.

Join me on this journey to see the errors of the liberal, woke agenda and learn how you can be part of a movement to preserve our cherished way of life. Together, we can ensure that the values and freedoms we enjoy today will still be there for future generations.

Chapter 1: The Immigration Debate

Introduction

Immigration is one of the most contentious and polarizing topics in contemporary politics. It's a subject that elicits strong emotions and opinions, often dividing families, communities, and nations. As a political analyst, author, and psychologist, I have delved deep into the intricacies of this debate, examining the historical context, current dynamics, and underlying psychological factors that drive the divergent views on immigration.

Historical Context

To understand the present, we must first look to the past. Immigration has been a defining feature of human civilization for millennia. From the ancient migrations that shaped early human societies to the mass movements of people during the industrial revolution, the flow of people across borders has played a crucial role in shaping the world we live in today.

In the United States, for instance, immigration has been a cornerstone of the nation's identity. The Statue of Liberty, with its famous inscription, "Give me your tired, your poor, your huddled masses yearning to breathe free," symbolizes the country's historical openness to immigrants. Throughout the 19th and early 20th centuries, millions of immigrants from Europe, Asia, and other parts of the world arrived in the United States, seeking better opportunities and contributing to the nation's economic and cultural development.

However, the welcoming attitude towards immigrants has not been consistent. There have been periods of intense xenophobia and restrictive immigration policies. The Chinese Exclusion Act of 1882 and the National Origins Act of 1924 are examples of legislative measures that sought to limit immigration based on racial and ethnic criteria. These historical ebbs and flows of immigration policy reflect the broader societal tensions and economic conditions of the times.

Current State of Debate

Fast forward to the 21st century, and immigration remains a hot-button issue. The debate is often framed in starkly binary terms: pro-immigration versus anti-immigration. However, the reality is far more nuanced. There are legitimate concerns and arguments on both sides, and understanding these perspectives is key to having a productive and informed discussion.

Pro-Immigration Arguments

Advocates for immigration often emphasize the economic benefits that immigrants bring to their host countries. They argue that immigrants fill labor shortages, contribute to innovation, and drive economic growth. For example, in the United States, immigrants have played a vital role in the tech industry, founding companies like Google, Tesla, and Intel. These companies not only create jobs but also contribute significantly to the economy.

Moreover, proponents highlight the cultural enrichment that immigration brings. Immigrants introduce new foods, traditions, and perspectives, fostering a more diverse and vibrant society. They argue that this cultural exchange is beneficial, promoting tolerance and understanding among different groups.

Humanitarian considerations also play a significant role in the pro-immigration stance. Many immigrants are fleeing war, persecution, and poverty, seeking safety and a better life for themselves and their families. Advocates argue that it is a moral obligation for wealthy, stable countries to provide refuge and support to those in need.

Anti-Immigration Arguments

On the other side of the debate, critics of immigration often focus on the potential negative impacts. They argue that high levels of immigration can strain public services, lead to job competition, and threaten national security. These concerns are not entirely unfounded and deserve careful consideration.

One of the primary economic arguments against immigration is the potential for job displacement. Critics argue that an influx of immigrants can lead to increased competition for low-skilled jobs, driving down wages and making it harder for native-born workers to find employment. This argument is particularly salient in times of economic downturn, when job scarcity heightens anxieties about job security.

Security concerns also feature prominently in the anti-immigration narrative. Critics argue that insufficiently vetted immigrants could pose a threat to national security, citing incidents of terrorism and crime involving immigrants. While it is important not to generalize or stigmatize entire groups based on the actions of a few, these concerns have a significant impact on public perception and policy.

Cultural preservation is another key argument for those opposed to immigration. Critics worry that high levels of immigration can lead to the erosion of national identity and cultural cohesion. They argue that if immigrants do not assimilate and adopt the values and customs of their host country, it could lead to social fragmentation and conflict.

Psychological Underpinnings

To fully grasp the immigration debate, it is essential to understand the psychological factors at play. Fear of the unknown, economic insecurity, and the desire for cultural continuity are powerful drivers of anti-immigration sentiment.

Fear of the unknown is a fundamental human instinct. When people encounter individuals who look, speak, and behave differently, it can trigger anxiety and suspicion. This fear is often exacerbated by sensationalist media coverage and political rhetoric that portrays immigrants as a threat. Understanding this psychological reaction can help explain why some people are more resistant to immigration.

Economic insecurity also plays a significant role. When people feel that their economic well-being is under threat, they are more likely to scapegoat immigrants. This is particularly true in communities that have experienced job losses and economic decline. In such contexts, immigrants can be perceived as competitors for scarce resources, leading to resentment and hostility.

The desire for cultural continuity is another important factor. People have a deep-seated need to belong to a community with shared values and traditions. When immigration leads to significant demographic and cultural changes, it can create a sense of loss and displacement. This is why some individuals and groups react strongly against immigration, fearing that their way of life is being threatened.

Humorous Touch

To illustrate the often absurd nature of the immigration debate, let's consider a fictional scenario. Imagine a town hall meeting where the topic of discussion is whether to allow a new wave of immigrants into the community. The meeting quickly descends into chaos, with participants shouting over each other, brandishing graphs and charts, and making outlandish claims.

One particularly vocal opponent stands up and declares, "If we let these people in, they'll take all our jobs and turn our town into a foreign country!" Meanwhile, a pro-immigration advocate counters, "But they make the best tacos! Do you really want to live in a world without tacos?"

Amidst the shouting, someone in the back raises their hand and says, "Can we all just agree that diversity is like a salad? A little bit of everything makes it better!" The room falls silent for a moment, as everyone contemplates the metaphor, before erupting in laughter. While humorous, this scenario underscores the complexity and emotional intensity of the immigration debate.

Conclusion

The immigration debate is multifaceted, with valid arguments on both sides. It is essential to approach the topic with an open mind, recognizing the economic, cultural, and humanitarian benefits of immigration while also addressing legitimate concerns about security, economic impact, and cultural cohesion.

In the next chapter, we will explore how immigration has led to significant cultural shifts in Western societies. We will examine the ways in which these shifts have both enriched and challenged the social fabric of host countries. Stay tuned, and remember: whether you're passionately pro-immigration or staunchly opposed, understanding the nuances of the debate is the first step towards meaningful dialogue and solutions.

Chapter 2: Cultural Shifts

Introduction

Imagine walking down the streets of any major Western city and hearing a symphony of languages, smelling the aroma of diverse cuisines, and seeing a blend of cultural attire. This paints a vibrant picture, doesn't it? But beneath this colorful surface, there lies a critical debate about cultural identity and national values. Together we will explore how immigration has led to significant cultural shifts, focusing on the need to preserve Western values and the challenges posed by certain immigration patterns. Let's delve into this complex issue with our eyes open.

The Melting Pot Myth

The romanticized notion of the "melting pot," where diverse cultures blend seamlessly into a harmonious whole, often oversimplifies reality. In many Western countries, the influx of immigrants has transformed cities into mosaics of distinct cultural enclaves, sometimes creating cultural friction rather than harmony.

Cultural Enrichment vs. Cultural Erosion

Immigration undeniably brings elements of cultural enrichment. New foods, festivals, music, and fashion can add vibrancy to society. Who doesn't love a good taco, sushi roll, or a Bollywood dance number? However, when the cultural differences are too stark and the values too divergent, it can lead to significant societal challenges.

The primary concern here is the erosion of national identity. When immigrants bring values that clash with the host country's core principles, it can strain social cohesion. This is particularly evident with immigration from Islamic nations, where certain cultural norms and legal principles, such as Sharia law, conflict sharply with Western values of freedom, equality, and secularism.

The Assimilation Imperative

At the heart of the cultural shifts debate is the need for assimilation. While it's enriching to have diverse cultural influences, it is crucial that immigrants adopt the core values and norms of their host country to ensure social cohesion. This means embracing the principles of democracy, gender equality, and freedom of expression, which are fundamental to Western societies.

Humorous Anecdote

To lighten things up, let's consider a humorous scenario: Imagine a British family inviting their new neighbors – an Indian family – for a traditional Sunday roast. The British family is eager to share their culture, while the Indian family, in turn, brings a spicy curry dish. The result? A hilariously spicy Sunday roast that leaves everyone gulping down water but also laughing and bonding over their culinary mishap. This story captures the essence of cultural exchange – it's enriching and bonding when done within the framework of mutual respect and shared values.

Economic Contributions vs. Cultural Costs

Immigrants undoubtedly make significant economic contributions. They bring new skills, fill labor shortages, and start businesses, driving economic growth. However, the cultural costs can sometimes outweigh these benefits if the values they bring are incompatible with the host society's norms.

For example, while immigrants from diverse backgrounds have bolstered industries like technology and healthcare, issues arise when communities resist integration. In some Western cities, enclaves have formed where the residents maintain their original customs and resist adopting the host country's language and laws, leading to social fragmentation.

Cultural Resistance and Fear

Resistance to cultural changes brought by immigration is often rooted in the desire for cultural continuity. People have a natural affinity for what is familiar and comfortable. When faced with significant cultural differences, it can trigger anxiety and defensiveness. This is especially true when those differences are perceived to undermine the host country's fundamental values.

The Role of the Media

The media plays a significant role in shaping perceptions of cultural shifts. However, there is a growing concern that mainstream media often downplays the challenges associated with immigration, particularly from Islamic nations. Instead of addressing the real issues, media outlets sometimes sugarcoat the problems and shift the blame onto the host nations, accusing them of racism and Islamophobia.

For instance, after terror attacks by Islamic extremists in Western countries, some media narratives have suggested that these acts were responses to the West's treatment of Muslims, rather than addressing the ideological motivations behind such acts. This kind of reporting can obscure the real issues and hinder productive discussions about integration and security.

Real-Life Incident

Consider the terror attacks in Western countries where the media has often deflected attention from the attackers' motivations. After the Manchester Arena bombing in 2017, some media reports focused on how the attack might fuel Islamophobia, rather than addressing the radical ideologies that inspired the attack. Similarly, the Charlie Hebdo attack in Paris was often framed as a reaction to offensive cartoons, rather than a violent assault on free speech and Western values.

By glossing over the ideological roots of such violence, the media fails to hold accountable those who promote extremist views and instead creates a narrative that places undue blame on the host society. This approach can undermine efforts to address the real challenges posed by certain immigration patterns.

Humorous Touch

Let's inject a bit of humor here. Imagine a news headline: "Local Man Horrified as Neighbour Cooks Spicy Food; Claims It Endangered His Pet Goldfish." While clearly an exaggeration, it captures how trivial cultural differences can be blown out of proportion and used to stoke fear, diverting attention from more serious underlying issues.

Policy Responses to Cultural Shifts

Governments have responded to these cultural shifts in various ways. Some have implemented policies aimed at promoting integration and social cohesion, while others have adopted more restrictive measures. For instance, Denmark has implemented stringent requirements for immigrants to adopt the national language and values, ensuring that newcomers integrate into the societal fabric.

Balancing Act

Finding the right balance between celebrating cultural diversity and ensuring social cohesion is a delicate task. It requires thoughtful policies that promote mutual respect and understanding. Education plays a crucial role in this process. Schools can foster an appreciation for different cultures while emphasizing the importance of shared values and norms.

Personal Stories

To illustrate the positive impact of cultural shifts, consider the story of Hamid, an immigrant from Syria who settled in Germany. Hamid started a successful bakery, introducing traditional Syrian pastries to his community. His bakery became a local favourite, and Hamid's story was featured in the local newspaper, highlighting how immigrants can enrich their new homes in unexpected ways.

Conclusion

Cultural shifts resulting from immigration bring both opportunities and challenges. While they can lead to tensions and fears about the erosion of national identity, they also offer the potential for cultural enrichment and economic growth. The key is to approach these changes with an open mind, recognizing the value of diversity while addressing legitimate concerns about integration and social cohesion.

In the next chapter, we will delve into the security concerns associated with immigration. We will examine both the real and perceived threats and discuss the policy responses to these concerns. Stay tuned for a balanced and insightful exploration of this critical aspect of the immigration debate.

Chapter 3: Security Concerns

Introduction

Imagine you're at a bustling airport, the anticipation of travel mingling with the slight anxiety of going through security. Now, amplify that tension to a national scale, and you have the crux of the immigration debate in many Western countries today. The integration of immigrants brings with it a host of security concerns. This chapter will dissect these issues with clarity, wit, and an eye towards preserving national security and Western values.

Real vs. Perceived Threats

Security concerns about immigration often get lumped into two categories: real and perceived. The challenge lies in distinguishing between the two without downplaying genuine risks or succumbing to unwarranted fear.

Real Threats

There is no denying that immigration can pose real security threats. This is particularly true when individuals or groups with radical ideologies exploit immigration policies to enter host countries. The rise in terror attacks across Europe and North America underscores this point. Incidents like the 2015 Paris attacks, the 2017 Manchester bombing, and the 2016 Berlin Christmas market attack highlight how extremist elements can infiltrate and operate within Western societies.

These tragic events have a common thread – the attackers often had connections to radical ideologies. Yet, the media and certain political voices frequently attribute these attacks to broader societal issues like xenophobia or social alienation, glossing over the ideological motivations. This misdirection hinders efforts to tackle the root causes of such extremism.

Perceived Threats

On the flip side, not all security concerns are grounded in reality. Some fears stem from misinformation or exaggerated narratives. For example, the notion that all immigrants from certain regions are potential criminals or terrorists is both inaccurate and counterproductive. It creates an atmosphere of distrust and fear that can further alienate immigrant communities, potentially driving vulnerable individuals towards radicalization.

However, it is crucial to acknowledge that dismissing all security concerns as mere paranoia is equally dangerous. The key is to approach these issues with a balanced perspective, ensuring that policies are based on evidence and effectiveness rather than fear or political correctness.

Media and Public Perception

The role of the media in shaping public perception of security threats cannot be overstated. Unfortunately, mainstream media often downplays or sugarcoats the challenges posed by certain immigration patterns. Instead of addressing the real issues, they frequently shift the blame onto host nations, accusing them of racism or xenophobia.

Consider the case of the Rotherham child sexual exploitation scandal in the UK, where media and authorities initially downplayed the severity of the problem due to fears of being labeled racist. This hesitation allowed the exploitation to continue unchecked for years, demonstrating the detrimental effects of not confronting the real issues.

Similarly, after various violent incidents involving immigrants, some media narratives suggest that these acts were responses to the host nation's societal issues, rather than addressing the individuals' ideological motivations. This kind of reporting can obscure the real issues and hinder productive discussions about integration and security.

Real-Life Examples

Consider the 2016 New Year's Eve incidents in Cologne, Germany, where groups of men, many of them immigrants, were involved in mass sexual assaults and robberies. Media coverage initially downplayed the immigrant aspect of the perpetrators, focusing instead on the societal reactions and potential backlash against immigrant communities. This narrative shift obscured the immediate security threat and delayed a focused response.

By glossing over these critical aspects, the media fails to hold accountable those who promote extremist views and instead creates a narrative that places undue blame on the host society. This approach can undermine efforts to address the real challenges posed by certain immigration patterns.

Policy Responses

Governments across the Western world have implemented various policy responses to address these security concerns. These measures range from enhanced vetting procedures to stringent border controls and surveillance programs.

Enhanced Vetting

One of the most effective ways to mitigate security risks is through enhanced vetting of immigrants. This involves thorough background checks, interviews, and scrutiny of an applicant's history and connections. While critics argue that this process can be invasive or discriminatory, it is a necessary step to ensure national security.

For example, the United States' vetting process for refugees includes multiple layers of checks conducted by various agencies, including the Department of Homeland Security, the FBI, and the Department of Defense. This rigorous process aims to identify and prevent individuals with radical ideologies from entering the country.

Border Controls and Surveillance

Another critical measure is the implementation of robust border controls and surveillance. Countries like Hungary have erected physical barriers to control the flow of immigrants, while others have increased surveillance at borders and within communities to monitor potential threats.

While these measures can be controversial, they are often justified by the need to protect citizens and maintain national security. The key is to balance these security measures with respect for individual rights and freedoms, ensuring that they do not lead to undue discrimination or profiling.

Community Engagement and Integration Programs

Beyond stringent security measures, it is essential to invest in community engagement and integration programs. By fostering a sense of belonging and inclusivity, host nations can help mitigate the factors that drive radicalization. Programs that promote language learning, cultural exchange, and economic opportunities can play a significant role in integrating immigrants into the broader society.

However, integration efforts must also emphasize the importance of adopting the host country's core values and norms. This includes respecting the rule of law, gender equality, and freedom of expression. By ensuring that immigrants understand and embrace these principles, societies can create a more cohesive and secure environment.

Balancing Act

Addressing security concerns related to immigration requires a delicate balancing act. It involves implementing effective policies that protect citizens while upholding the values and principles that define Western societies. It also requires a nuanced understanding of the real threats and challenges, as well as the need for inclusivity and respect for individual rights.

Humorous Touch

Let's inject a bit of humor here. Imagine a scenario where airport security introduces a new, foolproof method for vetting passengers – a truth serum. Passengers are asked ridiculous questions like, "Do you secretly enjoy pineapple on pizza?" or "Have you ever told your boss you're sick just to binge-watch Netflix?" While clearly a fantasy, this scenario underscores the need for thorough and effective vetting processes that go beyond the superficial.

Conclusion

Security concerns related to immigration are complex and multifaceted. They involve real threats that must be addressed through effective policies and measures. At the same time, it is crucial to avoid succumbing to unwarranted fears or discriminatory practices. By approaching these issues with a balanced perspective, societies can protect their citizens while upholding the values and principles that define them.

In the next chapter, we will explore the political responses to immigration. We will examine how different political parties and movements have addressed the issue and the impact of their policies on national identity and security. Stay tuned for a balanced and insightful exploration of this critical aspect of the immigration debate.

Chapter 4: Political Responses

Introduction

Picture a bustling political rally, flags waving, and a charismatic speaker riling up the crowd with fervent speeches about the need to protect national identity and security. Immigration is a polarizing issue, and political parties have crafted responses that reflect their ideologies and strategies for winning support. This chapter explores how different political parties and movements address immigration, the impact of their policies, and how these policies shape national identity and security.

Right-Wing Parties: Protecting National Identity

Right-wing parties have traditionally led the immigration debate, emphasizing the need to safeguard national identity and security. They argue that unchecked immigration can lead to cultural dilution and social fragmentation. Their policies often focus on strict immigration controls, enhanced vetting processes, and measures to ensure that immigrants assimilate into the host country's culture.

For instance, the Sweden Democrats, a right-wing party in Sweden, have gained substantial support by advocating for stricter immigration laws and promoting the idea that Swedish culture and values need protection from external influences. Their platform includes policies aimed at reducing immigration and encouraging immigrants to integrate fully into Swedish society.

Center-Right Parties: Balancing Act

Center-right parties often take a more moderate approach to immigration. They recognize the need for immigration controls to protect national security and social cohesion but also acknowledge the economic benefits that immigrants can bring. These parties advocate for balanced immigration policies that ensure security while promoting economic growth and social integration.

The UK's Conservative Party, for example, has implemented policies that tighten border controls and enhance vetting procedures while also emphasizing the importance of integrating immigrants into British society. They argue that a controlled and balanced immigration system is essential for maintaining social harmony and economic prosperity.

Liberal and Left-Wing Parties: Inviting Destruction

Liberal and left-wing parties generally adopt a more inclusive stance on immigration. They emphasize the humanitarian aspects, advocating for the rights of refugees and asylum seekers and promoting multiculturalism as a source of societal enrichment. However, these parties' policies can often be destructive to the host nation's cultural values and norms. They encourage individualism and so-called woke policies among the youth, promoting all manner of degeneracies and hedonistic tendencies.

Take, for example, the rise of pink and green-haired college students. These colourful hairdos seem to be a beacon for radical ideas. Almost overnight, these students become openly anti-Israel and anti-Semitic, waving banners in support of groups like Hamas. This dramatic shift can be attributed to the liberal media and the woke agenda, which shapes young minds to embrace radical ideologies. Influenced by a media narrative that often excuses violent behaviour and shifts the blame onto the host society, these students become vocal proponents of destructive ideologies.

Imagine a scene at a university campus where a group of these pink and green-haired students gather. With slogans that sound like they were concocted in a midnight dorm-room debate, they passionately advocate for causes they barely understand, fuelled by social media soundbites and sensationalist headlines. It's a humorous yet troubling sight, highlighting how easily impressionable young minds can be swayed by a skewed media narrative.

Populist Movements: Responding to Concerns

Populist movements across the globe have tapped into the genuine concerns of citizens about immigration. These movements often use straightforward language to address anxieties about cultural erosion, economic displacement, and security threats. By framing immigration as an urgent issue, populist leaders can galvanize support and push for necessary policy measures.

The rise of Italy's Lega Nord, led by Matteo Salvini, illustrates this approach. Salvini has effectively communicated the concerns of many Italians, positioning his party as the defender of Italian culture and security. His policies, such as closing ports to migrant boats and deporting undocumented immigrants, resonate with voters who feel their national identity and safety are at risk.

While some critics accuse populist movements of exploiting fears, it's important to recognize that these movements often bring to light valid concerns that mainstream parties might overlook. By addressing these issues head-on, populist leaders can foster a sense of empowerment among citizens who feel ignored or marginalized.

Impact of Immigration Policies on National Identity

Immigration policies significantly impact national identity. Strict immigration controls and assimilation policies aim to preserve cultural homogeneity and protect national values. However, they can also lead to social tensions and divisions if not implemented carefully.

In contrast, inclusive policies that promote multiculturalism and support for immigrants can enrich national identity by incorporating diverse cultural elements. However, if not managed well, they can also lead to perceptions of cultural dilution and social fragmentation.

Case Study: Denmark

Denmark provides an interesting case study of how immigration policies impact national identity. The Danish government has implemented stringent immigration policies, including strict requirements for family reunification, mandatory language classes, and cultural orientation programs. These measures aim to ensure that immigrants integrate fully into Danish society and adopt Danish values.

While these policies have been successful in promoting integration and reducing social tensions, they have also been criticized for being too harsh and exclusionary. Critics argue that the focus on assimilation can create barriers for immigrants and foster feelings of alienation.

Humorous Anecdote

To lighten the mood, let's imagine a political debate where candidates from different parties are asked to solve a fictional immigration crisis involving aliens from Mars. The right-wing candidate demands a space wall, the center-right candidate proposes a vetting system to ensure the Martians are friendly, the liberal candidate suggests welcoming them with open arms and learning from their advanced technology, and the populist candidate claims the Martians are here to take over the world and demands immediate action. While humorous, this scenario highlights the diverse and often conflicting approaches to immigration.

Policy Recommendations

Based on the analysis of various political responses, several policy recommendations can help balance the need for security and the benefits of immigration:

1. Enhanced Vetting Procedures: Implement thorough background checks and interviews to ensure that immigrants do not pose security risks. This can help prevent individuals with radical ideologies from entering the country while maintaining humanitarian commitments.

2. Integration Programs: Develop robust integration programs that promote language learning, cultural exchange, and economic participation. These programs should emphasize the importance of adopting the host country's core values and norms.

3. Community Engagement: Foster community engagement initiatives that build bridges between immigrants and native citizens. These initiatives can help reduce social tensions and promote mutual understanding and respect.

4. Balanced Media Reporting: Encourage balanced and responsible media reporting on immigration issues. Media outlets should strive to provide accurate and nuanced coverage that avoids sensationalism and fear-mongering.

5. International Cooperation: Engage in international cooperation to address the root causes of migration, such as conflict, poverty, and environmental degradation. By addressing these issues, countries can reduce the pressure of immigration and promote global stability.

Conclusion

Political responses to immigration vary widely, reflecting
the diverse ideologies and priorities of different parties and
movements. While right-wing parties emphasize the need
to protect national identity and security, liberal and left-
wing parties focus on inclusivity and humanitarian values.
Populist movements bring attention to genuine concerns
about immigration, addressing issues that mainstream
parties might overlook.

The challenge lies in finding a balanced approach that
addresses security concerns while recognizing the benefits
of immigration. By implementing thoughtful policies and
fostering community engagement, societies can navigate
the complexities of immigration and build a cohesive and
secure future.

In the next chapter, we will explore the media's role in
shaping public discourse on immigration. We will examine
how media narratives influence perceptions of immigration
and the impact of these narratives on policy and public
opinion. Stay tuned for a balanced and insightful
exploration of this critical aspect of the immigration debate.

Chapter 5: The Role of the Media

Introduction

Imagine the media as the conductor of an orchestra, wielding tremendous power to shape public perception and influence societal attitudes. In the context of immigration, the media plays a pivotal role, but often its influence is less about harmony and more about hitting the wrong notes. This chapter delves into how media narratives shape perceptions of immigration, sometimes distorting reality and impacting policy and public opinion. Let's explore this with a dash of common sense and a critical eye.

Media Narratives and Public Perception

The media holds a mirror to society, but it often decides which reflections to emphasize and which to blur. When it comes to immigration, the mainstream media has been accused of sugarcoating challenges and deflecting blame onto host nations. Instead of addressing the real issues, media narratives frequently shift the focus to racism or xenophobia, glossing over the complexities of integration and security.

The Glossing Over of Real Issues

Mainstream media often downplays or ignores the problems associated with certain immigration patterns. When incidents of violence or radical behavior occur, the narrative tends to emphasize the host society's supposed intolerance or systemic issues, rather than examining the ideological motivations behind these actions. This tendency to shift blame can create a distorted understanding of the immigration issue.

For instance, consider the case of the grooming gang scandal in Telford, UK. For decades, authorities and the media downplayed the severity of the issue due to fears of being labeled racist. This allowed the exploitation to continue unchecked, highlighting the detrimental effects of not confronting the real issues head-on.

Case Study: The Malmö Fireworks Incident

In a lesser-known but significant event, the city of Malmö, Sweden, experienced a series of chaotic New Year's Eve celebrations. Groups of youths, many from immigrant backgrounds, used fireworks as weapons, targeting police and civilians. Initial media coverage focused on the festive aspect of New Year's Eve and largely ignored the disturbing nature of these attacks. It wasn't until alternative media and local reports highlighted the severity that the public became aware of the actual situation. This narrative shift obscured the immediate security threat and delayed a focused response.

Humorous Anecdote

To lighten the mood, let's imagine a hilariously fictional scenario. Picture this: A small town newspaper headlines read, "Local Man Claims Alien Invasion After Neighbours Exotic Fruit Party." Turns out, Bob from down the street was convinced that an alien species had invaded Earth after seeing dragon fruits and rambutan at his neighbours housewarming party. Bob, armed with a colander on his head and a flashlight, stormed the neighbours yard, demanding they "return to their planet." It took the local sheriff and a lot of patience to explain to Bob that these "alien fruits" were just exotic imports from Southeast Asia. While everyone had a good laugh, it highlighted how easily the unfamiliar can be sensationalized and misunderstood.

Media's Influence on Youth: A Worrisome Trend

The media wields considerable influence over youth, shaping their worldviews and values. One particularly worrisome trend is how the media, combined with social media platforms, fosters radical ideologies and behaviors among young people. This influence can often lead them to adopt extreme viewpoints without fully understanding the complexities involved.

For example, there has been a noticeable rise in college students who suddenly embrace radical environmental activism. Influenced by viral social media campaigns and sensationalist media coverage, these students often engage in extreme protests, sometimes resorting to vandalism or violence. While environmental protection is crucial, the way these movements are portrayed and encouraged by the media can lead to dangerous actions.

Imagine a campus scene where students, inspired by a viral video, decide to chain themselves to trees on campus to prevent a hypothetical deforestation that isn't even planned. They chant slogans they saw online without fully grasping the local environmental policies or the actual issues at stake. It's a humorous yet troubling sight, highlighting how easily young minds can be swayed by a media narrative that oversimplifies and sensationalizes complex issues.

Balanced Reporting: The Need for Responsible Journalism

Balanced and responsible journalism is crucial in shaping a well-informed public. Media outlets should strive to provide accurate and nuanced coverage of immigration issues, avoiding sensationalism and fear-mongering. By presenting the complexities of immigration honestly, the media can foster a more informed and balanced public discourse.

Case Study: Responsible Reporting

Some media outlets have set positive examples by covering immigration issues with nuance and depth. For instance, certain investigative journalism pieces have shed light on the successful integration stories of immigrants who have contributed significantly to their host societies. These stories help balance the often negative portrayal of immigrants and highlight the potential for positive outcomes.

Policy Recommendations for Media Reporting

1. Promote Balanced Narratives: Media outlets should strive to provide balanced coverage that highlights both

the challenges and successes of immigration. This includes avoiding sensationalism and providing context to complex issues.

2. Encourage Diverse Voices: Including voices from different backgrounds and perspectives can enrich the narrative and provide a more comprehensive view of immigration issues.

3. Fact-Checking and Accountability: Rigorous fact-checking and holding journalists accountable for biased reporting can help maintain journalistic integrity and public trust.

4. Media Literacy Education: Educating the public, especially young people, on media literacy can empower them to critically evaluate news sources and narratives, reducing the influence of sensationalist and biased reporting.

Humorous Touch

Let's imagine a world where every news story is vetted by a "Truth-O-Meter" that buzzes loudly whenever a sensationalist or biased statement is made. Journalists would have to navigate through a minefield of buzzers, leading to a more careful and truthful reporting landscape. While fanciful, it underscores the need for greater accountability in media reporting.

Conclusion

The media wields significant power in shaping public perception of immigration. While it has the potential to inform and educate, it often falls short by sensationalizing or skewing narratives. By promoting balanced reporting and media literacy, society can foster a more informed and constructive public discourse on immigration.

In the next chapter, we will explore the future of Europe in the context of immigration. We will examine potential scenarios and policy responses to address the ongoing challenges and opportunities. Stay tuned for a balanced and insightful exploration of this critical aspect of the immigration debate.

Chapter 6: The Future of Europe

Introduction

Picture this: Europe, the land of Shakespeare, Da Vinci, and some seriously good cheese. A place where history meets modernity, and where every cobblestone street tells a story. But now, Europe stands at a crossroads, facing a wave of immigration that brings both opportunities and challenges. How will Europe maintain its rich heritage while navigating these changes? Buckle up, dear reader, as we dive into the future of Europe with a strong mind and a critical eye on maintaining traditional values.

Europe's Cultural Heritage: Why It Matters

Europe's cultural heritage is like a cherished family recipe passed down through generations. It's what makes Europe, well, Europe. Preserving these traditions isn't about being closed-minded; it's about valuing the unique tapestry that has shaped our identities. From the arts to our legal systems, these elements have been carefully woven over centuries.

Humorous Anecdote

Imagine Grandma's secret spaghetti sauce recipe. Now, imagine someone suggesting adding chocolate syrup to it. Outrageous, right? That's how many Europeans feel about blending radically different cultural practices with their own.

It's not about rejecting new ideas; it's about not ruining the sauce that's been perfected over time.

Traditional Values vs. Foreign Influences

Adopting foreign religions and cultural practices wholesale can sometimes lead to the erosion of our traditional values. This isn't about xenophobia; it's about understanding that not all cultural practices align with the principles that have built and sustained Western societies.

Take the increasing trend of Western women adopting Islam for love. Many do so under the belief that it offers a fair and equitable system. However, there are stark realities that often go overlooked.

Case Study: The Pitfalls of Idealizing Foreign Cultures

A growing number of Western women are converting to Islam, often influenced by romantic relationships. While the intentions are heartfelt, the reality can be sobering. Numerous reports highlight how these women face restrictive practices that clash with Western values of gender equality and individual freedom.

For instance, a BBC report documented the stories of Western women who converted to Islam and then found themselves trapped in oppressive situations, unable to leave the country or regain their previous freedoms. This isn't to say that all experiences are negative, but it underscores the importance of not romanticizing foreign cultures without understanding their full impact.

Why Keeping Traditional Values is Crucial

Our traditional values are the bedrock of our society. They foster a sense of identity, continuity, and stability. Embracing these values isn't about rejecting the new; it's about ensuring that the new doesn't erode the foundation that holds everything together.

The Future of Immigration in Europe

As Europe faces continued immigration, it's essential to approach the issue with clear-eyed pragmatism. This means establishing policies that balance humanitarian concerns with the need to protect and preserve cultural identity.

Policy Recommendations

1. Strict Vetting Procedures: Ensure that immigrants are thoroughly vetted to prevent the entry of those who do not align with European values of democracy, gender equality, and freedom of expression.

2. Integration Programs: Develop robust programs that help immigrants integrate into European society,

emphasizing the importance of adopting local customs and values.

3. Education on Western Values: Schools and community programs should educate both immigrants and natives about the importance of preserving Western values and the dangers of adopting practices that undermine these principles.

4. Support for Women: Specifically address the needs and rights of women who might be vulnerable to restrictive practices, ensuring they have access to support and resources.

Humorous Touch

Let's imagine a scenario where a group of aliens, fascinated by Earth's culture, decide to adopt human ways. They start dressing in tuxedos and eating with forks but insist on bringing their own bizarre customs, like greeting with headbutts. While it's hilarious to picture, it highlights the awkwardness and potential conflicts of blending fundamentally different cultural practices.

Conclusion

The future of Europe hinges on maintaining its rich heritage while navigating the complexities of immigration. By balancing openness with a firm commitment to traditional values, Europe can ensure its legacy continues to thrive. Embracing new ideas is important, but not at the expense of what makes Europe unique.

In the next chapter, we will explore the stark incompatibilities between Sharia law and Western norms, providing real-life examples of cultural clashes and emphasizing the importance of upholding secular values. Buckle up for a critical and insightful examination of this pressing issue.

Chapter 7: Sharia Law and Western Values

Introduction

Imagine a classroom where students are encouraged to ask questions, debate, and challenge ideas—a hallmark of Western education. Now, imagine a parallel classroom where questioning certain topics can result in severe punishment, and adherence to strict rules is mandatory. These contrasting environments highlight the fundamental differences between Western values and Sharia law. In this chapter, we'll explore the incompatibilities between Sharia law and Western values, providing real-life examples of cultural clashes and emphasizing the importance of upholding secular values.

The Incompatibility of Sharia Law with Western Norms

Sharia law, derived from the Quran and Hadith, governs many aspects of life, including politics, economics, and personal conduct. Its principles often conflict with Western norms, which are based on secularism, individual rights, and democratic governance. Here are some key areas of incompatibility:

1. Gender Equality: Western societies advocate for gender equality, promoting women's rights in education, employment, and personal freedoms. In contrast, Sharia law imposes strict roles and limitations on women. For example, in Saudi Arabia, women were only recently allowed to drive, and they still face significant restrictions in various aspects of life.

2. Freedom of Speech and Religion: Western values uphold the freedom of speech and the right to criticize any belief system, including religion. Sharia law, however, considers blasphemy a severe crime, often punishable by death. This stark difference was evident in the 2015 Charlie Hebdo attack in France, where journalists were murdered for publishing cartoons of the Prophet Muhammad.

3. Legal System and Punishments: Western legal systems are based on the principles of justice, fairness, and rehabilitation. Sharia law, on the other hand, includes harsh punishments such as amputations for theft and stoning for adultery. These practices are incompatible with modern Western legal standards.

Case Studies of Cultural Clashes

1. The Murder of Lars Vilks

Lars Vilks, a Swedish artist known for his controversial drawings of the Prophet Muhammad, was the target of multiple assassination attempts before his death in a car accident in 2021. Vilks lived under police protection for years due to the threats against his life, illustrating the severe danger faced by individuals who criticize or satirize Islam. His experiences underscore the peril that free speech advocates encounter when confronting radical ideologies.

2. The Garissa University College Attack

In April 2015, the militant group Al-Shabaab carried out a brutal attack on Garissa University College in Kenya. The attackers singled out non-Muslim students, killing 148 people and injuring many others. This horrific act of terror highlighted the dangers posed by radical Islamist ideologies and the severe consequences for those who do not adhere to their beliefs.

3. The Westgate Mall Massacre

In September 2013, Al-Shabaab militants attacked the Westgate shopping mall in Nairobi, Kenya, killing at least 67 people and wounding over 175. The attackers targeted non-Muslims, asking them to recite Islamic prayers to identify those they would execute. This attack underscored the global reach of Islamist terrorism and the threat it poses to public safety and multicultural societies.

Sharia Law in ISIS-Controlled Territories

In territories controlled by ISIS, Sharia law was enforced with brutal strictness. Women were forced to wear full veils, and those who violated dress codes faced severe punishments. Non-Muslims were forced to pay a protection tax (jizya) or convert to Islam. Public executions, amputations, and floggings were commonplace. The imposition of Sharia law in these areas created an atmosphere of fear and repression, demonstrating the harsh realities of living under such a legal system.

The Rise of Islamic Dawah Online

The rise of Islamic Dawah (proselytizing) online has been significant in spreading Islamic ideologies. Prominent figures like Ali Dawah and Mohammed Hijab have amassed large followings on social media platforms. These figures often present a sanitized version of Islam, downplaying controversial aspects such as gender inequality and strict Sharia punishments. They live comfortably in Western countries while promoting ideas that, if implemented, would undermine the very freedoms that allow them to speak openly.

Ali Dawah and Mohammed Hijab

Ali Dawah and Mohammed Hijab are known for their confrontational style and debates with critics of Islam. They often portray themselves as defenders of Islamic values while accusing their opponents of Islamophobia. Their narratives frequently include half-truths and misleading statements about the benefits of Sharia law and the supposed oppression of Muslims in the West. Despite their claims, they benefit from the freedoms and protections provided by secular, democratic societies.

If Immigrants Don't Like the Laws and Rules

If immigrants don't like the laws and rules in Western countries, they don't need to come. Western nations are built on principles of democracy, freedom, and equality, which are fundamentally at odds with Sharia law. If individuals wish to live under Sharia law, there are countries such as Iran and Afghanistan where it is enforced. The West must stand firm in upholding its values and not compromise on principles that ensure the freedom and rights of all its citizens.

The West Must Never Implement Sharia Law

Implementing Sharia law in any form within Western societies would be a grave mistake. The principles of Sharia are fundamentally incompatible with the values of democracy, freedom, and equality. Allowing any degree of Sharia law undermines the legal and cultural foundations that uphold human rights and personal freedoms. It is crucial to maintain a clear separation between religion and state to ensure that all citizens are treated equally under the law.

Conclusion

The challenges posed by the integration of Sharia law with Western values are significant and require urgent attention. By addressing these incompatibilities head-on, promoting fair and effective integration policies, and ensuring that Western values are upheld, we can protect our societies from the potentially destructive influences of radical ideologies. It's time to recognize and understand the real impacts of incompatible ideologies on our societies, ensuring that our approach is both compassionate and pragmatic.

In the next chapter, we will explore how immigration intersects with security and human rights. We will examine the challenges of ensuring national security while protecting the rights of individuals, and how these issues play out in policy-making. Join us as we navigate through this intricate and vital topic.

Chapter 8: Immigration, Security, and Human Rights

Introduction

Imagine a world where every country, from the most developed to the least, upholds human rights with the same vigor. Wouldn't that be something? Unfortunately, this isn't the reality. Often, developed nations are burdened with the responsibility of upholding human rights, while many other countries fall short. This disparity leads to a surge of asylum seekers, some genuine and some not, exploiting the systems of nations that prioritize human dignity. It's crucial to understand why human rights should be a global standard and not just a badge worn by developed nations.

Why Human Rights for All?

Human rights are fundamental and should be universal, ensuring that every individual, regardless of their country of origin, can live with dignity, freedom, and equality. When countries neglect these rights, it leads to suffering and drives people to seek refuge in nations that do uphold these principles. This often creates a strain on the host countries, as they must differentiate between genuine refugees and those exploiting the system for economic or other reasons.

Case Study: Exploitation of Asylum Systems

For example, there have been numerous cases where individuals from relatively stable countries have claimed asylum in developed nations like the United Kingdom or Germany, citing fabricated threats. These false claims not only strain the resources of the host countries but also undermine the plight of genuine refugees who desperately need protection. A notable case involved a group of Albanian nationals who sought asylum in the UK, claiming persecution that was later found to be unfounded. This misuse of the asylum system diverted attention and resources away from those truly in need.

The Security Concerns

Security concerns are often at the forefront of the immigration debate. While it's essential to protect national borders and citizens, it's equally important to approach these concerns with nuance and a commitment to human rights.

Real Threats vs. Perceived Threats

There are genuine security threats that need addressing, such as the risk of terrorism or criminal activities by a small minority of immigrants. However, it's crucial to differentiate between real threats and those exaggerated by fear and misinformation.

For instance, following several high-profile terrorist attacks in Europe, there has been a surge in security measures targeting immigrants. While these measures can help prevent genuine threats, they can also foster unwarranted suspicion and discrimination against entire communities.

Human Rights and Dignity

Balancing security with human rights is a delicate act. Ensuring that immigrants are treated with dignity and respect is fundamental to any just society. This means providing fair legal processes, humane living conditions, and protection from exploitation and abuse.

Case Study: Immigration Policies in Australia

Australia's strict immigration policies, including offshore detention centers for asylum seekers, have been heavily criticized for human rights abuses. Reports of poor living conditions, lack of medical care, and indefinite detention highlight the dangers of prioritizing security over human dignity. While aiming to deter illegal immigration, these policies often compromise the very values they seek to protect.

Security Measures and Integration

Effective security measures should not only protect but also facilitate the integration of immigrants. Integration programs that promote language learning, cultural exchange, and employment opportunities can help immigrants contribute positively to society and reduce security risks.

The Role of Law Enforcement

Law enforcement agencies play a crucial role in maintaining security while ensuring fairness. It is vital to be tough but fair with all residents within one's borders. This includes deporting illegal immigrants and migrants who have broken the law, without compromise. Taxpayers should not bear the cost of long-term imprisonment or rehabilitation for individuals who have violated immigration laws or committed crimes. This strict approach ensures that laws are respected and that the integrity of the immigration system is upheld.

Humorous Anecdote

Picture this: A small town decides to install high-tech security cameras at the local park to keep an eye on things. However, the cameras are so advanced that they start recognizing and greeting residents by name. One day, a new immigrant family visits the park, and the camera, confused, tries to strike up a conversation with their dog. The town ends up with hilarious footage of residents trying to explain the concept of dog ownership to a very polite but clueless camera. This light-hearted scenario highlights the importance of balancing security with a touch of humanity.

Human Rights and Immigration Law

Immigration laws must strike a balance between enforcing security and upholding human rights. Policies that dehumanize or discriminate against immigrants can lead to long-term societal harm and undermine the values of justice and equality.

Case Study: The Dangers of Overreach

In the United States, the Trump administration's "zero tolerance" policy led to the separation of thousands of children from their families at the border. This policy, aimed at deterring illegal immigration, faced widespread condemnation for its inhumane treatment of vulnerable individuals. It serves as a cautionary tale about the dangers of overreach in immigration enforcement.

Policy Recommendations

1. Balanced Security Measures: Implement security measures that protect against genuine threats while ensuring the humane treatment of immigrants. This includes thorough vetting processes and fair legal proceedings.

2. Integration Programs: Develop programs that help immigrants integrate into society, including language classes, employment assistance, and cultural orientation.

3. Tough but Fair Enforcement: Enforce strict laws to deport illegal immigrants and those who commit crimes. The state should prioritize deportation over long-term imprisonment, ensuring that the integrity of the immigration system is maintained without undue burden on taxpayers.

4. Humane Detention Practices: Ensure that detention facilities meet basic human rights standards, providing adequate living conditions, medical care, and legal assistance.

Conclusion

Balancing immigration, security, and human rights is a complex but essential task. By implementing thoughtful policies that protect citizens while upholding the dignity and rights of immigrants, societies can navigate these challenges effectively. Maintaining our values and commitment to human rights is crucial in building a just and secure future.

In the next chapter, we will explore the role of education in immigration, examining how schools and educational programs can facilitate integration and promote mutual understanding. Stay tuned for a balanced and insightful exploration of this critical aspect of the immigration debate.

Chapter 9: Immigration and the Role of Education

Introduction

Imagine a classroom filled with eager young minds from diverse backgrounds, all learning together and shaping the future of their community. Education is not just about imparting knowledge; it's about fostering understanding and integration. But here's the catch: if immigrants and their families don't want to live by the host country's standards and values, no amount of educational programs or well-intentioned integration efforts will make them productive members of society. Let's explore how education can bridge gaps and break down barriers—when there's willingness from both sides—and what happens when it doesn't.

The Importance of Willingness to Integrate

Education is a powerful tool for integration, helping immigrants learn the language, understand the culture, and navigate the social norms of their new country. However, this only works if immigrants are willing to adopt the host country's values and standards. Without this willingness, education alone cannot bridge the cultural divide.

Language Learning: The First Step

Learning the local language is the first and most essential step in integration. Without language skills, immigrants can struggle to access services, find employment, and fully participate in society. Schools play a vital role in providing language education to both children and adults, helping them communicate effectively and confidently.

Case Study: Language Programs in Canada

Canada, known for its multicultural approach, has implemented robust language programs for immigrants. These programs, available through public schools and community centers, offer free language classes to help newcomers integrate smoothly. The success of these programs is evident in the high levels of participation and the positive feedback from immigrant communities.

The Reality of Unwillingness

But what happens when immigrants are not willing to adopt the host country's values? Unfortunately, no amount of education can fix this fundamental issue. When immigrants resist integration, it often leads to negative outcomes, such as social isolation and economic hardship.

Case Study: The Challenges in Certain Neighbourhood's

Take the example of certain neighbourhood's in cities like Paris and London, where large numbers of immigrants have settled but have not integrated into the broader society. These areas often face higher crime rates, unemployment, and social tensions. For instance, the suburbs of Paris have seen numerous instances of unrest and violence, partly due to the lack of integration and adherence to local norms.

Cultural Orientation: Understanding the New Environment

Cultural orientation programs are equally important. These programs help immigrants understand the values, traditions, and social norms of their new country. They cover everything from legal rights and responsibilities to cultural practices and social etiquette. This knowledge helps immigrants feel more at home and reduces the risk of cultural misunderstandings.

Humorous Anecdote

Imagine a cultural orientation class where a group of new immigrants is learning about local customs. The instructor explains that in their new country, it's customary to make small talk about the weather. One enthusiastic student decides to practice this with everyone he meets, even the bus driver, the grocery store cashier, and the local police officer. His innocent but overzealous attempts to talk about the weather lead to some hilarious and heartwarming interactions, showing how learning new customs can sometimes lead to funny misunderstandings but ultimately brings people closer together.

The Negative Impact of Segregation

When immigrants live in the same neighbourhoods without integrating, it can lead to social segregation and a lack of cohesion. This often results in negative outcomes for both the immigrants and the host society. Segregated neighbourhoods can become hotspots for crime, economic stagnation, and cultural clashes.

Case Study: The Impact of Segregation in Malmö, Sweden

In Malmö, Sweden, certain districts have become heavily populated by immigrants who have not integrated into Swedish society. These areas face higher crime rates and economic challenges compared to other parts of the city. The lack of integration has led to social tensions and a feeling of disenfranchisement among both immigrants and native Swedes.

Promoting Mutual Understanding

Education doesn't just benefit immigrants; it also benefits the host society. Schools are a microcosm of society where children from different backgrounds learn and grow together. This environment promotes mutual understanding and respect, breaking down stereotypes and prejudices.

Involving Local Communities

Involving local communities in educational programs can enhance the integration process. Volunteer programs where local residents mentor immigrant families or help teach language classes can create bonds and foster a sense of community. These interactions help immigrants feel welcomed and supported, while locals gain a deeper understanding of the diverse cultures in their midst.

Challenges and Solutions

While the role of education in integration is clear, there are challenges to be addressed. Limited resources, language barriers, and differing educational backgrounds can hinder the process. However, innovative solutions can overcome these obstacles.

Case Study: Sweden's Introduction Program

Sweden has implemented an "Introduction Program" for newly arrived immigrants, which includes language classes, cultural orientation, and vocational training. The program also pairs immigrants with local mentors who help them navigate their new environment. This comprehensive approach has proven effective in helping immigrants integrate and contribute to Swedish society.

Policy Recommendations

1. Expand Language Programs: Invest in comprehensive language programs for immigrants, ensuring access to quality education for both children and adults. These programs should be flexible and accommodating to different learning needs and schedules.

2. Develop Cultural Orientation Courses: Implement mandatory cultural orientation courses that cover local customs, legal rights, and social norms. These courses should be tailored to the specific needs of different immigrant groups.

3. Promote Community Involvement: Encourage local communities to participate in mentoring and volunteer programs that support immigrant families. This fosters mutual understanding and strengthens community bonds.

4. Ensure Adequate Funding: Allocate sufficient resources to educational programs for immigrants, including training for teachers and support staff to handle the unique challenges of a diverse student body.

5. Enforce Integration Standards: Establish clear expectations for immigrants to adopt local values and standards. Those unwilling to integrate should face consequences, including potential deportation, to maintain social cohesion and respect for the host country's culture.

Conclusion

Education is a cornerstone of successful integration, but it requires willingness from both immigrants and the host society. By providing language education, cultural orientation, and promoting mutual understanding, schools and educational programs can help immigrants become active, contributing members of society—if they are willing to embrace their new home's values and standards. It's a win-win situation where both immigrants and the host society benefit, provided there is mutual respect and effort.

In the next chapter, we will explore the intersection of immigration, identity, and nationalism. We will examine how immigration impacts national identity and how societies can navigate these changes while preserving their core values. Stay tuned for a balanced and insightful exploration of this critical aspect of the immigration debate.

Chapter 10: Immigration, Identity, and Nationalism

Introduction

Imagine a grand old house that has been in your family for generations. It has its quirks and traditions, and everyone knows the rules: take off your shoes at the door, don't touch the antique vase, and always gather for Sunday dinner. Now, imagine inviting new people into this house—people with their own customs and traditions. How do you blend these different practices without losing the essence of what makes your house unique? This is the challenge that many Western nations face with immigration, as they try to balance national identity with the influx of new cultures. Let's delve into this issue with a clear-eyed focus on maintaining our values.

The Importance of National Identity

National identity is like the backbone of a country. It encompasses shared values, traditions, language, and history that bind people together. Without a strong national identity, a country can feel fragmented and directionless. Immigration, when managed well, can enrich a nation's culture. However, if newcomers do not adopt the host country's values and norms, it can lead to cultural erosion and social discord.

The Role of Integration

Integration is key to maintaining national identity while embracing the benefits of immigration. Immigrants who are willing to learn the language, understand the culture, and respect the laws of their new country can contribute positively to society. However, those who resist integration can create parallel societies, leading to tension and division.

Case Study: Integration Challenges in Germany

Germany has welcomed millions of immigrants over the past few decades. While many have integrated successfully, some communities have remained isolated, leading to challenges in social cohesion. For example, in certain neighbourhoods of Berlin, there are schools where German is rarely spoken, and cultural practices significantly differ from mainstream German society. This lack of integration has led to misunderstandings and, at times, conflicts.

Humorous Anecdote

Picture this: A town decides to host a "Cultural Fusion Day" where everyone showcases their traditions. One local family, proud of their heritage, sets up a booth to teach visitors how to play the traditional English game of croquet. Meanwhile, a newly arrived family from another culture sets up a booth right next to them, offering lessons in a high-energy martial art. The result? Croquet balls flying everywhere and confused participants trying to balance mallets and martial arts moves. The chaos ends in laughter, but it also highlights the importance of finding common ground and understanding each other's ways without clashing.

The Impact of Segregated Communities

When immigrants cluster in specific areas without integrating, it can lead to the formation of ghettos, where the residents' way of life remains entirely separate from that of the host country. This segregation can foster environments where host country laws and norms are ignored, and local values are overshadowed.

Case Study: Segregation in Dearborn, USA

Dearborn, Michigan, has one of the largest Arab-American populations in the United States. While this has brought a rich cultural diversity to the city, it has also created challenges. In some neighbourhoods, there is a significant separation between the immigrant community and the broader American society. This segregation has led to economic disparities, educational challenges, and social tensions. The lack of integration has resulted in parallel societies where cultural practices and values significantly differ from mainstream American norms, leading to misunderstandings and conflicts.

Nationalism: The Response to Integration Challenges

As integration challenges grow, so does the appeal of nationalism. Nationalist movements emphasize the importance of preserving national identity and prioritizing the interests of native citizens. While nationalism can sometimes veer into xenophobia, at its core, it is about maintaining the cultural and social fabric that defines a nation.

The Rise of Nationalist Movements

In many Western countries, nationalist parties have gained popularity by addressing the concerns of citizens who feel their culture and values are under threat. These parties advocate for stricter immigration controls, enhanced vetting procedures, and policies that ensure immigrants adhere to the host country's norms.

Case Study: The National Rally in France

The National Rally in France, led by Marine Le Pen, has gained significant support by promoting policies that protect French culture and values. They argue that immigration should be limited to those who are willing to integrate fully into French society. Their platform includes measures to reduce immigration and promote assimilation, reflecting a growing sentiment among the French that their national identity needs protection.

Humorous Anecdote

Imagine a neighbourhood meeting where long-time residents and new immigrants gather to discuss community issues. The long-time residents insist on traditional methods for decision-making, like raising hands and voting, while the new immigrants suggest using technology like apps for instant polls. The debate becomes a hilarious tug-of-war between old-school practices and new-age solutions, with one tech-savvy grandma stealing the show by managing to use both methods simultaneously. It highlights the need for balance and mutual respect in blending traditions.

Policy Recommendations

1. Enhanced Vetting Procedures: Implement thorough vetting processes to ensure that immigrants are willing to adopt the host country's values and norms. This includes background checks and interviews to assess cultural fit.

2. Mandatory Integration Programs: Develop comprehensive integration programs that include language classes, cultural orientation, and civic education. These programs should be mandatory for all new immigrants.

3. Community Engagement Initiatives: Foster community engagement by encouraging local residents to participate in mentoring and cultural exchange programs. This can help build mutual understanding and respect.

4. Support for National Identity: Promote policies that celebrate and preserve national traditions and values. This can include funding for cultural events, education on national history, and initiatives that highlight the importance of national identity.

5. Strict Enforcement of Laws: Ensure that all residents, including immigrants, adhere to the host country's laws.

Those who break the law should face appropriate consequences, including deportation if necessary, to maintain social order and respect for the legal system.

Conclusion

The intersection of immigration, identity, and nationalism is complex and often contentious. However, by focusing on integration and mutual respect, it is possible to embrace the benefits of immigration while preserving the cultural and social fabric that defines a nation. Balancing these elements is crucial for building a cohesive and prosperous future.

In the next chapter, we will explore the economic impacts of immigration, examining how immigrants contribute to the economy and the challenges that arise. Stay tuned for a balanced and insightful exploration of this critical aspect of the immigration debate.

Chapter 11: Economic Impacts of Immigration

Introduction

Imagine an old-fashioned lemonade stand on a hot summer day. The stand is bustling with kids, each with a specific role—one squeezing lemons, another adding sugar, and a third handling the money. Now, imagine a new kid joins the team. He's got fresh ideas and a different way of doing things. How will the lemonade stand adapt? Will the new kid help the stand sell more lemonade, or will his different methods create chaos? This is a simple way to think about the economic impacts of immigration. Let's dive into how immigrants contribute to the economy, the challenges that arise, and how we can stir the pot without spilling the lemonade.

Economic Contributions of Immigrants

Immigrants often bring diverse skills, fresh perspectives, and a strong work ethic, which can be a boon to the economy. They fill labor shortages, start new businesses, and contribute to innovation. In many Western countries, immigrants play a vital role in sectors such as healthcare, technology, and agriculture.

Boosting the Workforce

One of the most significant contributions of immigrants is their role in boosting the workforce. They often take on jobs that are hard to fill, from seasonal agricultural work to high-tech engineering positions. This not only helps keep the economy ticking but also supports industries that might otherwise struggle.

Case Study: Silicon Valley, USA

Silicon Valley is a prime example of how immigrants can drive economic growth. Many of the tech industry's leading companies were founded or co-founded by immigrants. Companies like Google, Tesla, and WhatsApp owe much of their success to the innovative minds of immigrants who brought new ideas and expertise to the table.

Humorous Anecdote

Picture this: A small town decides to hold a "Great British Bake Off" style competition. The town's best bakers are all set, but then a new immigrant family enters the contest. They bring in exotic ingredients and start baking a fusion cake that combines local flavors with their traditional recipes. The judges are initially skeptical—after all, who puts mango and chili in a Victoria sponge? But when the cakes are tasted, the fusion cake wins by a landslide. The town learns a valuable lesson: sometimes, fresh ideas can take the cake, literally and figuratively!

Economic Challenges and Misconceptions

While immigrants contribute significantly to the economy, their presence can also bring challenges. These include competition for jobs, pressure on public services, and the need for effective integration policies.

Job Competition and Wages

A common concern is that immigrants might take jobs away from native workers or drive down wages. While this can happen in certain sectors, most studies show that the overall impact of immigration on wages and employment is minimal. In many cases, immigrants complement rather than compete with the native workforce.

Strain on Public Services

Immigration can put pressure on public services such as healthcare, education, and housing. Effective policies are needed to manage these pressures and ensure that public services can cope with increased demand.

Case Study: The NHS in the UK

The UK's National Health Service (NHS) heavily relies on immigrant workers. Immigrants make up a significant portion of the NHS staff, from doctors and nurses to support staff. While their contribution is invaluable, the NHS also faces challenges in managing the increased demand for services. This dual impact highlights the need for balanced immigration policies that support both economic contributions and sustainable public services.

The Importance of Integration

For immigrants to contribute effectively to the economy, integration is key. Language skills, cultural understanding, and access to education and training are essential for helping immigrants become productive members of society.

Case Study: Integration Programs in Germany

Germany has implemented several integration programs aimed at helping immigrants learn the language, understand the culture, and find employment. These programs have shown positive results, with many immigrants successfully entering the workforce and contributing to the economy. However, challenges remain, particularly in ensuring that all immigrants have access to these opportunities.

Humorous Anecdote

Imagine a town where a new policy requires every resident to participate in a monthly "Cultural Exchange Day." One month, a local butcher and a newly arrived vegan chef are paired together. The butcher tries to explain the finer points of sausage making, while the vegan chef passionately talks about tofu. At first, there's a lot of awkwardness and misunderstanding, but by the end of the day, they've both learned a bit more about each other's world—and the butcher's shop even starts selling a new line of vegan sausages that become a local hit. This story highlights how integration, though sometimes comical, can lead to unexpected and positive outcomes.

Policy Recommendations

1. Supportive Integration Programs: Invest in comprehensive integration programs that provide language education, cultural orientation, and job training for immigrants. These programs should be accessible to all immigrants to help them integrate successfully into the economy and society.

2. Balanced Immigration Policies: Implement policies that balance the economic benefits of immigration with the need to manage public service demand. This includes ensuring that public services are adequately funded and staffed to handle increased demand.

3. Encouraging Entrepreneurship: Provide support and resources for immigrant entrepreneurs to start and grow businesses. This can include access to funding, mentorship programs, and networking opportunities.

4. Promoting Cultural Exchange: Foster initiatives that encourage cultural exchange and understanding between immigrants and native residents. This can help break down stereotypes and build stronger, more cohesive communities.

5. Effective Law Enforcement: Ensure that immigration laws are enforced fairly and consistently, with a focus on maintaining social order and respect for the legal system.

Conclusion

Immigrants bring invaluable contributions to the economy, from filling labor shortages to driving innovation. However, effective integration and balanced policies are crucial to maximizing these benefits while addressing the challenges. By fostering a welcoming environment and supporting immigrants' efforts to integrate, we can build a stronger, more dynamic economy.

In the next chapter, we will explore globalization and immigration, examining how global trends impact local cultures and economies. Stay tuned for a balanced and insightful exploration of this critical aspect of the immigration debate.

Chapter 12: Globalization and Immigration

Introduction

Imagine the world as a giant neighbourhood where everyone shares ideas, music, and sometimes even that annoying neighbours loud parties. This is globalization in a nutshell—a complex blend of cultures, ideas, and economies. But when it comes to immigration, globalization can be a double-edged sword. It brings opportunities but also challenges that impact local cultures and economies. Let's explore this fascinating intersection with our signature humor, wit, and a critical eye on maintaining traditional values.

Globalization: The Big Picture

Globalization has turned the world into an interconnected village. Trade, technology, and travel have brought us closer together than ever before. You can enjoy K-pop in New York, watch Bollywood movies in London, and shop for Italian fashion online from anywhere. But with these perks come significant challenges, especially regarding immigration.

The Good, The Bad, and The Complicated

Globalization has brought many benefits. It has expanded markets, increased access to goods and services, and fostered cultural exchange. However, it also poses challenges to local economies and cultures. The free movement of people means that immigration has become a hot topic, with opinions as diverse as the cultures it affects.

Humorous Anecdote

Picture this: A small town decides to embrace globalization by hosting an international festival of sports and games. The festival organizers decide to include a mix of traditional local games and international sports. So, you have a tug-of-war team from the local school facing off against a group of enthusiastic Japanese sumo wrestlers. Then there's the traditional three-legged race, but with competitors on stilts inspired by a South African tradition. It's hilariously chaotic as the townspeople try to navigate these new, unfamiliar games, leading to lots of laughs and a few harmless tumbles. While the festival was a fun experiment in globalization, it highlighted how mixing too many diverse elements can sometimes lead to cultural confusion rather than enrichment.

Economic Impacts of Immigration

Globalization has a profound impact on economies, and immigration plays a significant role in this process. Immigrants often bring diverse skills, fresh perspectives, and a strong work ethic, which can be a boon to the economy. However, the influx of people also brings challenges, such as job competition and pressure on public services.

Boosting the Workforce

One of the most significant contributions of immigrants is their role in boosting the workforce. They often take on jobs that are hard to fill, from seasonal agricultural work to high-tech engineering positions. This not only helps keep the economy ticking but also supports industries that might otherwise struggle.

Case Study: The Role of Immigrants in Agriculture in California, USA

California's agricultural sector heavily relies on immigrant labor. Immigrants make up a significant portion of the workforce in fields such as fruit picking, vegetable farming, and dairy production. Their contributions are essential for maintaining the supply chain and ensuring that fresh produce reaches consumers. However, this dependence also highlights the need for fair labor practices and the importance of recognizing the vital role immigrants play in the economy.

Cultural Exchange and Integration

While economic contributions are crucial, the cultural exchange facilitated by globalization is equally important. Immigrants introduce new traditions, foods, and perspectives that enrich the local culture. However, successful integration requires willingness from both immigrants and the host society to embrace these differences.

Why Is Nobody Flooding Into the Middle East and North Africa?

It's a curious phenomenon that migration traffic predominantly flows from Africa and Islamic countries to the West rather than the other way around. Several factors contribute to this one-way traffic, primarily revolving around issues such as political instability, lack of human rights, and economic challenges in these regions.

Political Instability and Corruption

Many countries in Africa and the Islamic world suffer from political instability and corruption. Governments are often authoritarian, with little regard for democratic principles or human rights. This creates an environment where citizens feel unsafe and oppressed, leading them to seek refuge in more stable and democratic nations.

Religious and Social Restrictions

Strict religious laws and social norms in many African and Islamic countries restrict personal freedoms. Issues like gender inequality, limited freedom of speech, and harsh penalties for dissent make these countries unattractive for both their citizens and potential immigrants. In contrast, Western countries offer greater personal freedoms and a more inclusive environment, making them more desirable destinations.

Economic Challenges and Low Levels of Education

The economic opportunities in many African and Islamic countries are limited compared to those in the West. High unemployment rates, low wages, and limited access to quality education further drive people to seek better lives elsewhere. Western countries, with their robust economies and educational opportunities, present a stark contrast.

Case Study: The Syrian Refugee Crisis

The Syrian refugee crisis exemplifies these issues. Millions of Syrians have fled their country due to civil war, seeking safety and stability in Europe and North America. They are escaping not just the violence, but also the lack of opportunities and freedoms in their homeland. This mass exodus highlights the disparities in living conditions and the reasons behind the one-way migration flow.

Policy Recommendations

1. Help Nations Develop Economically: Instead of focusing solely on integrating immigrants into Western societies, it's essential to help their home countries become economically successful. This involves genuine, non-exploitative development aid, investment in infrastructure, and support for democratic institutions. Western nations should collaborate with international organizations to provide comprehensive development plans. For instance, the UN's Sustainable Development Goals (SDGs) provide a framework for addressing poverty, inequality, and education.

2. Promoting Political Stability and Good Governance:
Western countries can support political stability and good
governance in developing nations through diplomatic
efforts and by funding programs that promote transparency
and accountability. This includes training programs for
government officials and supporting anti-corruption
initiatives. For example, the World Bank's Governance and
Institutional Development Division offers programs aimed
at strengthening public sector management and fighting
corruption.

3. Encouraging Education and Skill Development:
Investing in education and vocational training in
developing countries can help create a skilled workforce
that drives economic growth. Western nations can fund
scholarships, build schools, and support teacher training
programs. Organizations like UNESCO and the Global
Partnership for Education are already working towards
improving educational outcomes in developing countries.

4. Supporting Local Entrepreneurship: Encouraging
entrepreneurship in developing nations can stimulate
economic growth and create jobs. This can be done
through microfinance initiatives, business development
services, and access to global markets. The International
Finance Corporation (IFC) and other entities offer financial
products and advisory services to support small and
medium-sized enterprises (SMEs) in developing countries.

5. Promoting Fair Trade Practices: Western nations should
advocate for fair trade practices that allow developing
countries to compete in the global market without being
exploited. This includes reducing trade barriers, providing
fair prices for goods, and ensuring ethical labor practices.
Organizations like Fairtrade International work to promote

these principles and support farmers and workers in developing countries.

Conclusion

Globalization and immigration are complex phenomena that bring both opportunities and challenges. By balancing openness with a commitment to traditional values, societies can navigate these complexities and build a cohesive and prosperous future. However, it is equally important to address the root causes of migration by helping developing nations become economically stable and politically secure. This not only benefits the countries in need but also contributes to global stability and reduces the pressure on immigration systems in the West.

In the next and final chapter, we will explore the darker side of immigration, focusing on incompatible ideologies and religious practices. We'll delve into the potential threats these pose to Western values and societal norms. Stay tuned for a critical and insightful examination of this pressing issue.

Chapter 13: The Dark Side of Immigration: Incompatible Ideologies and Practices

Introduction

Imagine a neighbourhood barbecue, where everyone brings their favorite dishes, and there's an unspoken rule that you don't double-dip in the communal guacamole. Now, imagine someone new joins the barbecue, bringing their own food and customs, which is great—until they start insisting that everyone else change how they eat. Suddenly, the barbecue is in chaos. This analogy, though light-hearted, mirrors the serious challenges faced by Western nations due to immigration policies that have failed to address incompatible ideologies and practices. Let's dive into the darker side of immigration with a critical eye on preserving our values.

The Nightmare of Unchecked Immigration

Destruction of Local Communities

There are numerous cases where local communities have been significantly altered, often for the worse, due to immigration policies that prioritize inclusivity over integration. For example, Rotherham in the UK became infamous for the child sexual exploitation scandal where predominantly Pakistani grooming gangs abused over 1,400 children between 1997 and 2013. The authorities, afraid of being labeled racist, ignored and downplayed these crimes, leading to a prolonged nightmare for the victims.

Rise in Crime and Terrorism

The rise in crime and terrorism in Western countries has been partly attributed to immigration from regions with differing cultural and religious norms. The Bataclan Theatre attack in Paris in 2015, where Islamic State terrorists killed 130 people, is a stark reminder of how dangerous ideologies can slip through the cracks of liberal immigration policies. Furthermore, the New Year's Eve assaults in Cologne, Germany, where over 1,200 women were sexually assaulted by groups of men of North African and Arab descent, highlighted the authorities' inability to manage the situation effectively.

Unprosecuted Hate Speech

In many Western countries, hate speech and incitement to violence within certain communities are often ignored or inadequately prosecuted. Radical imams preaching hate and violence in mosques have continued their activities under the guise of religious freedom. For instance, Anjem Choudary, a British Islamist social and political activist, spent years promoting extremist views and recruiting for ISIS before finally being convicted in 2016. His activities were overlooked for too long, causing significant damage.

Media Bias and Double Standards

The media often plays a significant role in shaping public perception. When crimes are committed by immigrants, especially those from Islamic backgrounds, there is a noticeable reluctance to cover these stories extensively.

However, when attacks are perpetrated against immigrants or Muslims, these incidents are widely publicized. For example, the media coverage of the Christchurch mosque shootings in New Zealand was extensive and immediate, as it should be. However, less attention is given to incidents like the Charlie Hebdo shooting or the stabbing spree in Reading, UK, where the attackers were motivated by Islamic extremism.

The Sinister Agenda of Liberal Woke Movement

The liberal woke movement often promotes an agenda that undermines Western values under the guise of inclusivity and tolerance. By pushing for policies that allow unchecked immigration and promoting narratives that paint any criticism as racist or xenophobic, they effectively silence reasonable discourse and critique. This approach creates an environment where discussing the real impacts of immigration becomes taboo, allowing harmful ideologies to fester.

Case Study: The Murder of Theo van Gogh in the Netherlands

Theo van Gogh, a Dutch filmmaker and outspoken critic of Islam, was brutally murdered in Amsterdam in 2004 by Mohammed Bouyeri, a Dutch-Moroccan Muslim. Van Gogh had directed a controversial film, "Submission," which criticized the treatment of women in Islamic societies. His murder was a chilling wake-up call about the dangers of radical ideologies. Bouyeri shot van Gogh multiple times, attempted to decapitate him, and left a note pinned to his body with a knife, threatening further attacks. This incident highlighted the extent to which radical Islam can penetrate Western societies and silence free speech through terror.

The Atrocities Faced by Christians and Jews in Islamic Countries

Christians and Jews living in many Islamic countries face systemic discrimination, persecution, and violence. This grim reality is often overlooked by the international community, which prefers to focus on promoting religious tolerance. However, the facts speak for themselves. In countries like Pakistan, blasphemy laws are frequently used to target Christians and other religious minorities. Accusations often lead to mob violence, and the accused can face the death penalty.

In Egypt, Coptic Christians have faced church bombings, kidnappings, and forced conversions. The government's response has been largely inadequate, with perpetrators rarely brought to justice. The 2017 Palm Sunday church bombings in Tanta and Alexandria killed over 45 people, yet these attacks are just a fraction of the ongoing persecution faced by the Coptic community.

The Violent Spread of Islam

Islam spread rapidly after the death of Muhammad in 632 AD, largely through violent conquest and jihad. The early Islamic caliphates expanded their territories through wars and invasions, subjugating vast regions in the Middle East, North Africa, and beyond. This expansion was not a peaceful process; it involved the slaughter of thousands, the imposition of Islamic rule, and the forced conversion of conquered peoples.

The concept of jihad, or holy war, was a central tenet in this expansion. The early Muslim conquests, often glorified in Islamic history, were marked by brutal tactics and the suppression of other religions. This violent history is a stark reminder of the potential consequences when radical ideologies are left unchecked.

The Consequences of Inaction

If Western societies continue on the current trajectory, ignoring the warning signs and failing to address the incompatible ideologies that some immigrants bring, we risk seeing our own societies mirror the chaos and repression found in many Islamic countries and parts of Africa. This includes the erosion of women's rights, the suppression of free speech, and the rise of religiously motivated violence.

Shocking Evidence from Jihad Watch

The website Jihad Watch provides a sobering look at the real impacts of radical Islamic ideologies infiltrating Western societies. Here are some chilling examples:

1. Increased Terror Attacks: The rise in terror attacks across Europe, from the London Bridge attack to the bombings in Brussels, showcases the growing threat. These attacks are often carried out by individuals who

have been radicalized within their communities, demonstrating a failure to integrate and adopt Western values.

2. Cultural Clashes: In countries like Sweden and Germany, there have been numerous reports of cultural clashes, including violent crimes and sexual assaults, perpetrated by immigrants from Islamic backgrounds. These incidents often go underreported or are downplayed to avoid accusations of racism.

3. Silencing Dissent: Critics of Islam, like Ayaan Hirsi Ali and Salman Rushdie, have faced death threats and violence for speaking out. Their experiences underscore the peril of allowing radical ideologies to flourish unchecked, as they not only threaten individual lives but also the foundational principle of free speech.

The Dire Consequences of Inaction

If Western societies continue on the current trajectory, ignoring the warning signs and failing to address the incompatible ideologies that some immigrants bring, we risk seeing our own societies mirror the chaos and repression found in many Islamic countries and parts of Africa. This includes the erosion of women's rights, the suppression of free speech, and the rise of religiously motivated violence.

Conclusion

The challenges posed by unchecked immigration and the promotion of incompatible ideologies are significant and require urgent attention. By addressing the root causes of migration, promoting fair and effective integration policies, and ensuring that media coverage is balanced and responsible, we can protect Western values and societal norms while supporting global stability and prosperity. It's time to look beyond the surface and understand the real impacts of immigration on our societies, ensuring that our approach is both compassionate and pragmatic.